Schiphol

Schiphol

AMSTERDAM'S
AIRPORT
BELOW
THE
SEA

MARC DIERIKX

Airlife
England

First published in the UK in 1999
by Airlife Publishing Ltd

**British Library Cataloguing-in-
Publication Data**
  A catalogue record for this book
  is available from the British Library

ISBN 1 84037 062 9

Typeset by Rowland Phototypesetting Ltd,
Bury St Edmunds, Suffolk.
Printed in Hong Kong.

Airlife Publishing Ltd
101 Longden Road, Shrewsbury, SY3 9EB,
England
Telephone: 01743 235651 Fax: 01743 232944
E-mail: airlife@airlifebooks.com

Cover:
A KLM Asia Boeing 747-400 taxies to its
holding position before take-off.

Back cover:
Passengers exiting from the airport
building.

Halftitle page:
Façade of Schiphol's Terminal West.

Title page:
General view of the landside of the
terminal.

Preface

Schiphol has been in use as an international airport since 1920, but its history goes back four more years. During this long period, the airport has gone through several turbulent phases in which its existence was threatened. It has, however, emerged from these problems time and time again to become one of Europe's foremost international airports, renowed for its passenger comfort.

This book combines Schiphol's history in a nutshell with a glimpse of the airport's present-day operations. It seeks to provide some background to the difficulties encountered in Schiphol's development, as well as to offer some explanation of the ever-fascinating spectacle of airport and airline operations today.

This book could not have been made without the kind assistance of a number of people at Schiphol who provided me with access to the airport and answers to my various questions. To all of them I owe my gratitude. I would particularly like to mention Ed Ploegstra, Assistant Manager Marketing and Communications, who supported the project with enthusiasm, and Marjolein van de Vaart and Bernadette Pluis of Schiphol's Hostess Service, who guided me on my photographic quest and made sure that I did not disappear into any jet engine in the process.

Marc Dierikx

A short history of Schiphol Airport

Like most airports until the mid-1920s, Schiphol was little more than a military airfield, unequipped for airline use. When the first aircraft landed in September 1916, a military Farman F-22, Schiphol started out as an auxiliary base for the Netherlands' Air Corps. Military needs dictated Schiphol's location close to defensive fortifications in the otherwise near-empty Haarlemmermeer polder south-west of Amsterdam, a former inland sea once renowned as a place where ships sank. The sea gave Schiphol its name and also dictated the airport's location: west of the area the Dutch had prepared to inundate to halt invading armies, should the Great War spill over to Dutch soil. It was intended that Schiphol be used as a starting point for reconnaissance flights to monitor enemy troop movements east of the Water Line. Local conditions at Schiphol were less than ideal for aircraft, but the land was cheap and that was what mattered at the time. Located thirteen feet (four metres) below sea level, Schiphol's topsoil was waterlogged. In subsequent years drainage continued to be a problem and in wet periods Schiphol's landing field lacked sufficient strength to support the increasingly heavy commercial aircraft.

The first civil flight touched down on Schiphol's soggy turf on 17 May 1920. A de Havilland DH16 of Air Transport & Travel Ltd brought two British journalists, the morning editions of *The Times* and the *Daily Mail* and a letter from the Lord Mayor of London to the Burgomaster of Amsterdam. It expressed the wish that air services would further trade and commerce between the two cities. The aircraft took off for London the next day, carrying a small bag of Dutch airmail. It did so on charter to KLM (Koninklijke Luchtvaart Maatschappij – Royal Dutch Airlines), founded seven months before on 7 October 1919 and home carrier at Schiphol ever since.

In the early years amenities at Schiphol were few. Apart from a small wooden KLM hotel just outside the airport's

---

1920s

perimeter, the only structures found on the airport were intended to house aircraft. Access to the airport was also a problem. Surface transport, other than the KLM bus service for passengers from Amsterdam's city centre, was not available. Passengers arriving from Amsterdam by car had to cross two toll bridges before they came to the narrow wooden structure spanning the canal that encircled the Haarlemmermeer polder. Once across the bridge, Schiphol was situated at the end of a gravel road. Even on a good day, the 11.5 kilometres from Amsterdam took over thirty minutes.

Initially, developments at Schiphol were slow. In the first five years of airline operations a single civil hangar sufficed for the night parking of aircraft, maintenance and passenger and cargo check-in until in April 1926 the city of Amsterdam took over the management of the airport from the military. This was the outcome of a process of negotiations dating back to the days of the first airline services. It was realised early on that conditions at Schiphol were inadequate for a means of transport hoping to attract a clientele of affluent passengers. At the same time the Amsterdam municipal authorities were convinced that the airport, if improved, would have a stimulating effect on the city's economy in the long term. In this respect, Amsterdam had a key role to play, although straightening out the various legal and financial implications of transferring the airport from the Ministry of Defence to the city took years. Thus began the transformation of the muddy airfield with its wooden hangars into a real airport. This process was helped by public acclaim of the first return flights between Amsterdam and the capital of the Dutch East Indies, Batavia (Jakarta), in 1927. Departing on 15 June, a single-engined Fokker FVIIa, chartered from KLM by the American millionaire Van Lear Black completed the one-way journey in a leisurely thirty-eight days. Eleven weeks later, on 1 October a three-engined Fokker FVIIa-3m mailplane also departed for Batavia, but needed only twenty-two days to return.

With the 1928 Olympics on the horizon, Amsterdam initiated the construction of a modest terminal building at Schiphol in order to improve check-in facilities, which had hitherto been taken care of in a draughty corner of the KLM hangar. The wooden plank platform in front of the KLM hangar was also replaced by a larger concrete apron. The landing ground was levelled and its drainage system improved. To help pilot orientation, the middle of the landing field was now marked with a big white circle. Pilots were further aided on their final approach by a large aircraft-shaped wind indicator placed in a corner of the landing area. It could be lighted in case of night operations. Radio connections and weather forecasting for airmen were also upgraded.

However, the airport's location near Amsterdam meant that Schiphol lacked centrality to the other large population centres in Holland's western provinces. In the absence of good road connections to the major cities that made up the area's *Randstad* conurbation and to the rest of the country, KLM's managing director, Albert Plesman, felt its growth potential was constrained. Plesman never tired of lobbying for the construction of a new airport that would be more centrally located. By the mid1930s these efforts resulted in a nationwide discussion on the ideal location of an airport to serve the Dutch air transport needs. That location, Plesman maintained, was not Schiphol, but a site near the city of Leiden, favourable to the construction of road and rail connections. Although the new airport never made it off the drawing-board, the discussions that ensued from Plesman's plans lasted for over a decade. They were not finally resolved until 1949, when the government decided to shelve all plans for a new international airport.

Despite the economic crisis of the 1930s, Amsterdam set about improving Schiphol as far as municipal finances would allow. Boosted by the public enthusiasm for the results that KLM's brand-new Douglas DC-2 *Uiver* brought home from the Melbourne Race, the city improved the landing ground from 1934 onwards. To provide a lasting solution to the problem of soil condition, a system of hard-surface runways was built in 1937–8.

The new runways spearheaded a number of techno-

Early 1930s

logical changes in the airport's environment. Concrete runways necessitated changes in approach procedures, as landing aircraft had to be positioned precisely in line for touchdown. The problems involved with this were tackled by incorporating runway and approach lighting systems into the design and construction of the new runways. Studies were also undertaken on how to improve Schiphol's radio beacon and use this to bring aircraft on course for landing. Air traffic control facilities were also upgraded, promoting Schiphol's importance as the air traffic control centre for flights crossing Dutch airspace.

In 1936 the terminal was enlarged to provide space for the growing number of passengers using the airport, while a new hotel was constructed just outside Schiphol's perimeter for the increasingly demanding air traveller. With these facilities Schiphol became one of the best equipped airports in Europe – a model that was even followed elsewhere. The plans also provided for improved integration with the Dutch road infrastructure through direct access to the Amsterdam–The Hague motorway then under construction. The total pre-war city investments at Schiphol amounted to approximately seven million guilders.

These investments were lost in the events following the German invasion of the Netherlands. In the early hours before dawn on 10 May 1940, Schiphol was the primary target for the first bombing raid in the German campaign against its neutral neighbour. Most of the bombs hit the area adjacent to the apron, where KLM's orange-painted aircraft formed targets that could easily be identified. After only five days of war, the Dutch were forced to surrender. Consequently, Schiphol became a *Luftwaffe* airbase, home to bomber and fighter squadrons that lashed out against Britain in the first two years of the war. When the German war effort shifted east, squadrons of night-fighters arrived, as Schiphol was strategically located on one of the main bomber routes to Germany.

As the bomber offensive increased, so did Schiphol's military significance. This was demonstrated by a massive raid against the former airport on 13 December 1943, in which 199 American B-26 bombers 'marauded' the airport's runways and structures to such an extent that the Germans decided to withdraw their remaining aircraft and personnel from Schiphol. In the final year of the war the abandoned airport formed the backdrop for destitute city dwellers looking for firewood amid the rubble to keep warm.

After 1945 the rapid resurgence of KLM placed pressure on Dutch airport planning. Following emergency repairs to the runways in the first months after liberation, a number of wooden shacks were erected to serve as airport buildings until the construction of a new terminal could be finished.

Hangars were also badly needed: in the first post-war year aircraft maintenance had to be carried out in the open air. Even under these primitive conditions, KLM set about rebuilding its network. KLM's first intercontinental flight, an ex-military Douglas C-54 Skymaster bound for Batavia, took off from Schiphol on 28 November 1945. Services with refurbished C-47 Dakotas to London and other European cities were gradually reopened from December 1945 onwards. Airport planning, however, went beyond the reconstruction of the old facilities. Under the guidance of Schiphol's director Jan Dellaert (1893–1960) the Amsterdam Department of Public Works designed a Plan for the Expansion of Schiphol Airport, which Dellaert presented early in 1949.

The design provided for the construction of a new airport right next to the existing one. Six to ten runways were envisaged, pointing in different wind directions from a central terminal area. This tangential layout, imitating the designs of the leading airports in the United States, New York's Idlewild and Chicago's O'Hare, made it possible to blend part of the old runway structure with the new airport. Depending on the final arrangement, either one or two of the old runways would be integrated as the most cost-effective way to expand Schiphol's traffic capacity. Even so, the estimated cost of the new airport went beyond the means of city finance. In 1949 the total cost of the project was estimated at 167.5 million Dutch guilders. It was clear from such figures that the decision-making process would take time, and that the Government would have to step in to foot the bill.

Apart from financial reasons, there were also political grounds for the Government to become directly involved in the airport planning process. With the increasing significance of air travel, the importance of Schiphol extended beyond the municipal interests of Amsterdam to a national level. In post-war international aviation politics, the Netherlands had to negotiate bilateral trade-offs of landing rights with third countries. Also, in the 1950s the expansion possibilities for KLM became linked to Schiphol's appeal as a destination for foreign airlines. In this respect the Dutch considered a well-equipped airport

1950s

an important factor in discussions on landing rights. Time and again this necessitated technological changes at Schiphol to continue its ranking among the world's best airports.

Between 1949 and 1957 the plan for the new airport made its slow and cumbersome way through the Dutch planning bureaucracy. The decision to go ahead with its construction on the basis of the grand plan of 1949 was not finalised until 1956, when both Amsterdam and the Government acceded to a downscaled version of the original design, comprising four runways only. The tangential concept was, however, rooted so deeply that no fundamental changes in the future layout were attempted and this concept remained the cornerstone of the new Schiphol.

While the plans were under review technological advances continued, to which Schiphol adapted its operational facilities. In the first post-war years the airport welcomed the installation of new runway lighting systems to guide aircraft on their final approach. Schiphol co-operated with the Netherlands Civil Aviation Authority in drawing up specifications for improvements in the sphere of radar and air traffic control. For passengers, a new semi-permanent terminal opened in 1949, some months after the official presentation of the plans for the new airport. With these plans in mind, facilities were kept as small as possible. This necessitated near-continuous adaptations and expansions of the terminal to keep pace with the growing numbers of air travellers. In 1949 Schiphol catered for 263,654 passengers; ten years later their annual number surpassed the one million mark for the first time and reached 1,134,787. The main waiting room repeatedly proved too small and had to be expanded in 1953, 1955, 1957, 1961 and again in 1965. However, it was clear by 1965 that the new airport facilities, construction of which had commenced in January 1963, removed the financial logic of expanding the existing ones.

The most rapid developments, however, were in the area of cargo transport. Partly because of the modest size of the Dutch passenger market, partly because of KLM's approach to air transport, the Dutch carrier built Schiphol's growth on a combination of passenger and cargo transport, the latter developed especially quickly. Between 1946 and 1953 the volume of KLM's cargo traffic increased ten times faster than the airline's passenger traffic: 14.3 million tonnes in 1952 (an increase of 658% compared to 1946), against a 65% increase in passenger numbers over the same period. For that reason the airline opened a cargo centre in 1952. It was purpose-built by Schiphol and rented to KLM as the first of its kind in Europe, pre-dating the construction of similar buildings at other European airports by a decade. After several expansions towards the end of the 1950s, when Schiphol had become Europe's number three cargo airport (after London-Heathrow and Paris-Orly), the development of cargo transport was further aided by the opening of a Customs *entrepot* in 1963. Goods flown in from abroad and destined to be re-exported, could now be stored in a special warehouse within the Customs area until they continued their onward journey. For the shipping and handling companies and the airlines, this saved considerable paperwork.

In 1957, ten years after the design was conceived, work was commenced on the first runway on the new Schiphol. Because the scale of the investment brought Government involvement to all aspects of airport operation, a new legal and organisational structure for the running of Schiphol became necessary. At the end of a ten-year struggle between the Government and Amsterdam about who would control the new airport company, the Articles of Foundation were signed in January 1958. They reflected the tenacity with which Amsterdam's negotiators had defended the city's vested interest in Schiphol. Despite the changed ownership structure, Amsterdam would, through appointees on a Supervisory Board, maintain a significant influence on the course of Schiphol's development.

Building the new airport took another ten years. In the two decades during which the airport took shape, developments in aviation turned out to be very different from what the small group of planning experts had imagined in 1947. The introduction of the Caravelle, Boeing 707, and Douglas DC-8 passenger jet aircraft in the 1950s, the first of which arrived at Schiphol in 1956, dramatically changed the technological system of commercial aviation. On the one hand, the introduction of large and expensive jets made the airlines steer towards the development of mass air travel. Airport planning had to prepare for a significantly higher traffic growth than had previously been assumed. On the other hand, the jets brought a new set of planning problems in the shape of noise nuisance. The combined effects of these demonstrated the fundamental gap between the developments of aircraft technology and airport construction. Yet, a review of the layout for the new Schiphol Airport, to take the noise issue into account, did not take place. Such a review would have resulted in serious delays in the construction of the new airport. Time-consuming changes in design and construction would have affected Schiphol's attractiveness as a port-of-call for foreign airlines.

On the assumption that it would only be a matter of time

before the evolution of aircraft and engine technology would provide a solution to the noise problem, Schiphol was finished according to plan, despite words of warning from noise experts. Although Schiphol's surrounding municipalities were informed about the consequences of the construction of the new runways and their use by jet aircraft, an absence of a clear understanding of the problems to be encountered meant that housing projects around the airport continued. The harmony between the airport and its surroundings, which had characterised Schiphol's development until the end of the 1950s, thus came under pressure.

Late 1950s

On 15 January 1963 work was commenced on the construction of the central terminal area. By then the terminal design had shrunk as a result of the recession caused by the costs involved in introducing the first generation of jet aircraft. A financial crisis held the airline industry in its grip from 1961 to 1963. In 1956 the design for the new airport had provided for a terminal with fifty-seven gates. In the light of events at the beginning of the new decade that number was reduced to twenty-five. Even so, construction costs rocketed. If the original calculations of 1949 reckoned with a total of 9.5 million guilders for the terminal, the actual cost of the building in 1967, despite its reduced size and capacity, amounted to just over ten times that figure. However, if the terminal was considerably over budget, its size and capacity – six million passengers annually – soon turned out to be too small. Within six months of the new airport opening on 28 April 1967, plans had to be implemented to expand the terminal to an eventual annual capacity of sixteen million passengers in anticipation of the Jumbo jet's arrival. As a first phase, the southern pier of the terminal was to be expanded with a secondary waiting room area and docking facilities for five wide-body aircraft. Thus in 1971, Schiphol's capacity increased to eight million, which was still not enough.

Indeed, the growth of aviation was such that it became doubtful whether Schiphol would be able to continue serving as the nation's airport. Between 1968 and 1972 passenger traffic forecasts for the year 2000 increased from predictions of an annual 55 million to figures in the order of 104 million. To prepare for this rapid growth of air travel, both the government and Schiphol's Board of Directors initiated studies on the future air transport infrastructure in the Netherlands. By the end of the 1970s they had each arrived at their own conclusions. The Government appeared to favour the construction of a second national airport, which would be more able to cope with the expected traffic increase than Schiphol's alternative of building an additional runway and adding a second terminal area.

In both plans the key issue was noise nuisance. In the 1960s, the arrival of large numbers of jet aircraft a

Schiphol had brought to light the fundamental flaw in the airport's layout. The four runways, designed to ensure maximum operational efficiency by providing optimal opportunities for headwind take-off and landing, meant that jet noise fanned out in all directions around the airport, affecting a great number of people. The Dutch decision-makers had been late to recognise the severity of this problem and when they did they found that little could be done to avoid it. The problem was, of course, not specific to Holland. Increasing public protests against jet noise marked a general shift in the public's perception of airports. As well as focal points for the remarkable technology of flight, airports now also became focal points for protests against the intrusion aircraft made on the everyday lives of those living in the vicinity of an airport.

After protracted studies, the Dutch discovered that there were two options open to reduce the annoyance . They could either construct a new airport where aviation would be able to grow without repercussions on its environment, or adapt the existing airport in such a way that it could grow within reasonable noise annoyance limits. The first alternative was the most expensive, as it not only involved designating a location for a new airport that would hinder no-one and the construction of the new airport itself, but also the necessary surface infrastructure. This proved prohibitively expensive. The matter became even more complex when it was found that in a small and densely populated country like the Netherlands, a suitable location could not be found on dry land and would have to be reclaimed from the water.

By the end of the 1970s, discussions about the second national airport had settled on a single location, the envisaged Markerwaard polder in the IJssel Lake east of Amsterdam. However, when the Government faced the need to make a final decision, the airline industry was moving towards a recession after the surge of oil prices since 1973. On the basis of the accordingly lowered forecasts of that time, the price for the second national airport was considered too high. Although no formal decision to abandon the Markerwaard Airport was made, preparations stopped in 1979 after the Cabinet decided that a new airport would not be necessary before the year 2000.

This brought Schiphol's alternative, first proposed in 1968, back into the limelight. Schiphol proposed the construction of a fifth runway in the relatively empty polder to the west of the airport, parallel to the existing pair of north-south oriented runways. Although the airport's plans originated in the very high traffic forecasts of the late 1960s and early 1970s, the Board of Directors later found that the new runway also made sense from an environmental point of view. It could contribute to a reduction of the existing noise levels in the urbanised areas beneath the flightpath of the other runways. In the noise-driven debate on the future of Schiphol, and of airport planning as such, this was an important asset. Recognition of Schiphol's importance to the national economy did the rest. In the 1980s and early 1990s the fifth runway plan survived extensive public debate on the future of Schiphol. After nearly three decades of discussions on noise and environmental issues, Schiphol received the official go-ahead in 1995.

Schiphol's perseverance in championing the fifth runway was indicative of the Board's long-term strategy to push Schiphol into the top echelon of European airports. According to forecasts in the mid-1980s, world air transport routes would gravitate towards a limited number of primary nodes, from which smaller airports would be served. This process, which originated in the United States as *hubbing*, favoured the 'naturally large' airports in Europe, such as those of London and Paris. As German's primary international airport, Frankfurt also featured as a probable candidate to develop into a major *hub*. For Schiphol, with its geographically limited hinterland, such a development was less likely, and for this reason the airport developed its own policy aimed at pushing it into the top league of European airports. This involved a perspective of the functions of an airport, and these were redefined in a much broader fashion than had been the case before. Schiphol's growth, voluminous reports said, should be geared towards integrating air, rail and road transport and attracting the development of light industrial and office parks for businesses with close ties with the airport, or with air transport as such. This strategic concept was confirmed in the airport's Masterplan Schiphol 2003 of 1989. In the Dutch terminology (borrowed from English usage), Schiphol was to become a 'mainport'. To achieve this coveted status an ambitious programme for the expansion and development of the airport and its facilities was set up.

Such ambitions, however, meant that the airport was increasingly criticised by environmental protection groups, who observed the unbridled growth of the air transport industry with distrust. Here again, the effects of Schiphol's general layout in the densely populated western part of Holland were evident. The number of people affected by aircraft noise and air pollutants from aircraft engines was relatively high. The Board of Directors recognised the severity of the noise-related problems and initiated several programmes to reduce annoyance. Probably the most important of these was a programme for the insulation of several thousand houses in the areas most affected by aircraft noise. Prevention of complaints now also moved up the agenda. Continuous noise monitoring led to new procedures for landings and take-offs, aimed at reducing Schiphol's noise contour.

Despite Schiphol's willingness to enter into discussions with its opponents about a stated double goal of growth and a reduction of nuisance, the critics of the plans for growth were not appeased. As a result of public participation and political pressure in 1995 the further growth of Schiphol was tied to a ceiling of 44 million passengers and 3.3 million tonnes of cargo in the year 2015 and within specified noise limits.

However, the development process put in motion with the mainport strategy was such that the actual growth of air traffic at Schiphol in the second half of the 1990s turned out to be significantly higher than had been predicted a few years earlier. As a result, in 1997 special exemption measures had to be taken by the minister for Traffic and Waterworks to allow Schiphol to meet the rising demand for take-off and landing slots within the legal standards of the noise limits. It transported the conflict between economic and environmental interests to the front pages of the Dutch newspapers. It has remained there since, awaiting the construction and opening of the fifth runway and the outcome of ongoing discussions about constructing a new subsidiary airport in the shallow coastal waters offshore.

While the planning discussions continued, the airport went through a period of many physical changes. By the time the annual capacity of the terminal opened in 1967 had been expanded to 16 million passengers in 1975, the growth of air transport at Schiphol showed signs of stagnation. In 1977, plans for a scheduled second terminal were shelved as high oil prices took their effect. The plans re-emerged again in 1989 as part of a new overall strategy to adapt the airport to the needs of the twenty-first century. That year the Board of Directors presented its Masterplan Schiphol 2003, which provided for a second terminal, connected to the original building in such a way that the two terminals would merge into one single structure. As the plans progressed, ideas about this structure developed and took on the form of the airport's prided One Terminal Concept. In this plan the two terminal segments would be united by a covered Schiphol Plaza that blended the existing forecourt with a new underground rail terminal and an airport shopping mall.

The shopping mall itself was the outcome of a long process of reviewing airport management, the first seeds of which had been sown in the late 1950s. In 1957 Schiphol became one of Europe's first airports to have stalls offering tax-free goods for sale to passengers. During the subsequent decade Schiphol successfully developed tax-free concessions into an additional source of income and when the new airport opened in 1967, its terminal provided for a number of tax-free shops. However, in 1995 Schiphol Plaza went one step further, introducing regular high street shops, food courts and even a supermarket in the landside section of the terminal, where both flying and non-flying visitors to the airport would be encouraged to shop. The increase in non-aeronautical revenue was stimulated further by real estate development, most visibly in the opening of a World Trade Centre in front of the terminal in 1996.

Schiphol has traditionally been strong in the field of cargo transport. In this respect the airport was helped by its home carrier, KLM, which early on emphasised its double role as a passenger and cargo airline. After the first specialised cargo building had been handed over to KLM in 1952, the growth of freight traffic was such that it warranted the construction of a new cargo terminal in the 1960s as part of the new airport facilities. It was opened in

1967, along with the rest of the new airport. In the subsequent years, the cargo terminal had to be doubled to keep up with growth.

The rapid increase of air cargo was a general phenomenon in international air transport after 1970, and Schiphol targeted this field for further development. Since the 1970s Schiphol has used its location in north-western Europe, as well as a number of special provisions for easy interchange of air and road cargo, as an asset to attract foreign cargo airlines. In the 1980s the airport played a prime role in marketing Holland as the 'Gateway to Europe' for transport companies worldwide.

These general efforts were focused on technological improvements. The airport and the air cargo companies operating at Schiphol joined forces to create a computerised cargo check-in system in 1983, called Cargonaut. It was subsequently linked to a Customs declarations system in 1987, thus enabling the automatic processing of the complicated loading, import and export forms. Such developments boosted the appeal of Schiphol as a port of call for international cargo airlines and road-aid cargo hauliers. Business developed to the point where, in 1993, a new cargo station could be opened in the southern part of the airport for use by KLM's competitors.

Yet, the most important changes for Schiphol's long-term development probably took place underground. To provide the new Schiphol with a rail link had been on the agenda right from the first 1947 concepts for the new airport. However, a hesitant Government, which had other financial priorities, and the recurrent doubts of airport planners as to whether air travellers might actually be potential train travellers, had prevented Schiphol being linked to the national rail network at the time the new airport was being built. Indeed, it was with some difficulty that the Netherlands Railways were able to secure permission from the Government, in advance of the decision-making process, to construct a partial underground rail terminal and a section of railway tunnel underneath one of the new runways at the time when the new airport was built.

Faced with increasing road congestion because of the growth of private car ownership, however, the Government revoked its position in May of 1973. After many years of deliberation, the cabinet now agreed to the construction of a railway line between Amsterdam and The Hague via Schiphol, where an underground railway station would be built. Because a large section of the rail link had to pass underneath the airport, it was decided to build a 6.5-kilometre long tunnel. This would be made of watertight caissons sunk into a long trench dug across the airport's soggy ground. The first trains stopped underneath Schiphol's air terminal in 1981. However, full integration of the rail link with the national network was not achieved until June 1986, when intercity train services commenced between Amsterdam's Central Station and The Hague. This integration made it possible for public transport to achieve an approximate 30 per cent share of the surface passenger traffic to and from the airport.

With an eye on the future where both air traffic capacity, road congestion and environmental concerns might become limiting factors in airport growth, in the 1990s the airport and the Netherlands Railways decided to upgrade the underground station as part of an overall reconstruction of the airport terminal facilities. After the expensive project was completed in 1995, Schiphol was hooked up to Europe's growing network of international high-speed trains in 1996.

Below: Schiphol, aerial city of glass: travellers' view of aircraft parked at the G-pier from the corridor that connects the central parking deck with the terminal.

Opposite: Schiphol's landside shopping centre, 'Schiphol Plaza'. Only the control tower is a reminder that this is an airport, not a regular shopping mall.

Above: Schiphol is situated four metres (13 feet) below sea level, symbolised by the airport's artwork in Terminal West. Blue plastic 'waves' represent the true water level, should the dykes fail, while the orange 'tropical fish' underneath them refer to destinations far away to which the traveller is about to depart. Down below, waiting passengers bide their time seated at 'coral reef' benches, while a KLM MD-11 awaits boarding at gate F3.

Opposite: In the new terminal West, opened in 1995, Schiphol has tried to create a relaxed environment with a number of artful distractions intended to remove passenger anxiety.

Left: Artwork can be found at various locations in the airport and throughout the terminal in an effort to lure the passengers' thoughts away from the dynamic world of global air travel, captured here in fluorescent lights. In the background a Northwest Airlines' (NWA) Boeing 747-400 and a Douglas DC-10 are readied for departure.

Below: There *are* other things to watch at Schiphol besides aircraft. Another prominent feature is the tax free shopping centre. Shopping has a long history at Schiphol, going back to the second half of the 1950s. Since then, the stalls have continuously been expanded and updated, creating a shopping mall environment for tax free purchases, although from 1999 restricted to those travelling outside the European Community.

Opposite below: Flight KL611 to Chicago O'Hare rapidly climbs out to cruising altitude above the North Sea. The transatlantic alliance between KLM and NWA preceded a Dutch-American bilateral civil aviation agreement in 1992 which provided for open skies between the two countries, granting carriers unrestricted access to each other's airports. The co-operation between KLM and Northwest stimulated the growth of air traffic at Schiphol.

Left: Northwest Airlines' flight 39 lifts off from Schiphol's northerly runway 01L for its non-stop flight to Boston's Logan International Airport. Through code-sharing the flight doubles as flight KL8039. Since KLM came to the aid of the then ailing American carrier in 1989, the alliance between them has served as a model to follow throughout the international airline industry.

Right: The formation of international airline alliances has been one factor in the increasing number of daily flights to and from Schiphol. Another important factor has been the trend towards hub-and-spokes operations in the airline business. Schiphol features as a central node where traffic from many different European airports is assembled and where passengers are redistributed to continue their journeys to intercontinental destinations, and vice versa. The increasing number of flights is evidenced in the growing number of departures listed on television screens throughout the terminal complex. To the average passenger the number of destinations and departure gates can be daunting.

Below: Transfer, not only of passengers but also of cargo, has become of growing importance to Schiphol. For passenger transfer the airport features numerous desks where air travellers are pointed in the right direction to find their connecting flight.

Below: Operating both propeller aircraft, like these Fokker 50 turboprops, and smaller jets such as the Fokker 70, KLM Cityhopper offers flights to a range of destinations on so-called 'thin' routes, which do not warrant the use of KLM's standard medium-range jets of the Boeing 737 series.

Above: Although passengers for the smaller propeller aircraft enjoy the same kind of facilities available to those who travel to intercontinental destinations, boarding is still carried out in the traditional fashion at the apron. The large windows, one of Schiphol's prominent features, offer a good view of the activities and movement outside.

Below: KLM is the biggest user of Schiphol for flights to intercontinental destinations. Passengers wait to board one of the airline's fleet of thirty Boeing 747s.

Opposite above: Loaded with fuel, cargo and passengers to its maximum take-off weight of 377,800kg, KLM's PH-BUK *Louis Blériot*, a Boeing 747-306 Combi, awaits clearance for take-off at the threshold of runway 01L. Twenty-two of KLM's thirty Boeing 747s are of the mixed passenger and cargo configuration. Their forward cabins and upper decks seat from 273 (Boeing 747-400) to 297 passengers (Boeing 747-300).

Opposite below: In 1988 KLM took a shareholding in Britain's regional carrier Air UK. Since then Air UK has grown into Schiphol's second biggest user after KLM, boosting Schiphol's function as a major hub in European air traffic. After acquiring all shares of Air UK in 1997, KLM renamed its British subsidiary KLM UK in 1998.

Below: To increase brand visibility, a programme was started in 1998 to respray all Air UK aircraft in the colours of a new regional subsidiary. Photographed half-way through the process, this ATR 42 awaits passengers for its return flight to Humberside. The forward hatch gives access to the aircraft's luggage compartment.

Above: KLM's other regional partner is the German carrier Eurowings, which operates services to Schiphol from Cologne, Dortmund, Dresden, Düsseldorf, Hanover, Leipzig, Nuremberg, Paderborn and Stuttgart, mainly using ATR turboprop aircraft.

Left: A Suckling Airways Dornier Do 228, just arrived from Cambridge, is marshalled into position on the apron in front of B-pier, where regional flights are handled. Larger aircraft dock at the piers themselves, most of which are equipped with Visual Docking systems that allow the pilot to steer the aircraft to its exact parking position, ready for hook-up to a passenger loading bridge.

Below: For aircraft parked on the apron, power to maintain the aircraft's systems and air-conditioning is provided by mobile generators.

Above: Since airport operations have been organised according to the hub-and-spokes concept, aircraft arrive and depart in waves. In the late afternoon a Maersk Air Boeing 737-500 arrives from Billund on the Danish west coast with passengers bound for various destinations.

Above: With dusk setting, a Fokker 50 is on finals for touchdown on runway 06. For business people flying from regional airports, KLM Cityhopper offers so-called dawn/dusk connections between Schiphol and regional airports.

Above: After sundown, airport operations continue. Hooked up to a 400Hz electrical power unit that has come to replace the aircraft's noisy and polluting Auxiliary Power Units as a source of electricity, a KLM Boeing 737 is readied for boarding. In the background, SAS's daily MD-80 evening flight to Copenhagen is nearly ready for pushback.

Opposite: A Swissair Airbus A320 is parked and cleaned at gate E4 for its 20.30 service to Zürich.

Below: Late in the evening Schiphol becomes quieter after the last flights to the Far East have departed. In the morning, charter flights are among the first to take off, maximising aircraft utilisation. One of Transavia's Boeing 737-300s is cleaned for an early flight to the sunny Mediterranean.

Below: Most large airports in Europe suffer from road congestion and Schiphol is no exception. The answer to this has been the construction of an underground railway station, fully hooked up to the Dutch intercity train network. Over 28 per cent of the total number of passengers arrive at the airport by public transport. Schiphol even has a TGV-service to Paris.

Opposite above: Airport operations continue in all weather conditions. After a rainstorm a KLM Boeing 747-400 decelerates after landing on runway 06.

Opposite below and above: Jets of water nearly hide the aircraft as thrust reversers blow water in all directions.

Above: Heavy use necessitates thorough maintenance. Schiphol-East features a number of very large maintenance hangars that fit aircraft of all sizes. After a month of operation, KLM's Boeing 747-400 *City of Seoul* undergoes its periodical check-up in bay 2 of hangar 12.

Left: Not only the aircraft need work, as Schiphol itself is constantly undergoing changes. Since 1993 the airport has had to adapt to the new regime of non-passport border crossings between the 'EU countries'. After building a second level on Schiphol's E-pier, operational deployment of 'EU-traffic' and 'non-EU traffic' also necessitated the construction of a new basement for automated baggage handling. Schiphol's location below sea level means that digging a hole in the ground immediately produces water. Special techniques have been developed to pour concrete under submerged conditions.

Left: One of the building projects under way is the construction of a new satellite terminal facility. Preparations for construction have been carefully planned not to hinder regular operations. As an Aeroflot Tu-154M waits for clearance to taxi to the terminal, a KLM MD-11 proceeds to runway 01L. The difference in size of the two trijets is clearly visible.

Below: For its afternoon flight to Bucharest, a TAROM Boeing 737-300 takes off from Schiphol's 01L, or 'Zwanenburg' runway. TAROM, short for Transporturie Aeriene Romana, has always had a preference for Boeing aircraft. In the foreground, building companies have taken up temporary residence to work on Schiphol's next expansion phase.

Above: After the break-up of Yugoslavia, the number of Balkan carriers at Schiphol increased as the new republics all sprouted their own airlines. On a rainy morning a Croatia Airlines' A320 from Zagreb is on final approach to runway 27.

Opposite above: Even before the nose-wheel of this Iberia McDonnell Douglas MD-87 has touched the ground, the pilot has its engines in thrust-reverse position to decelerate the aircraft.

Opposite below: While the last passengers deplane from TAP Air Portugal's Airbus A310, personnel from Aero Groundservices, one of three handling companies at Schiphol, move a loader under its cargo hatch.

Above: Off! Transavia flight HV605 leaves for its scheduled service to London–Gatwick. Originally a charter operator, Transavia diversified into scheduled services in the early 1980s.

Above: A closer look at Transavia's playful colour scheme, as flight HV605 begins its climb to cruising altitude.

Below: A Lufthansa Airbus A320 passes one of KLM's MD-11s, waiting to receive its 'cargo train' at gate F7.

Above: Although Schiphol has imposed financial discouragements aimed at reducing the use of noisy 'Chapter 2' aircraft, banning all noise-makers has not been possible. Aeroflot is but one of the airlines that has continued to rely on the older generation of jets, like this Tupolev Tu-134A, the prototype of which first flew in 1965.

Opposite: One of the unusual features that sets the Tu-134 apart from western airliners, is its glass nose, offering extra downward visibility for landings at airports without sophisticated instrument landing systems. Newspapers read on the long flight from Moscow litter the floor.

Above: From the same era, the BAC 1-11 has survived as a regular visitor at Schiphol. British Airways continues to use several of these aircraft on its services between Birmingham and Amsterdam, their engines fitted with 'hush-kits' to reduce noise emissions.

Right: With daily flights between Kiev and Amsterdam, Ukrainian International Airlines has become a regular customer at Schiphol. After pushback from gate G-9, the air and ground crews complete their checklist before taxying.

Above: Not all airlines from the newly independent states that once made up the Soviet Union have been financially strong enough to complete the expensive change-over to Western equipment. Lithuanian Airlines continues to use the Yakovlev Yak-42 trijet on the route between Vilnius and Amsterdam.

OO-DWB

Sabena

Opposite above: A Turkish Airlines' Boeing 737-400 makes a pretty sight against the clouds, as it retracts its undercarriage and climbs from runway 01L to begin its flight to Istanbul.

Opposite below: Early in 1998, KLM and Northwest expanded their alliance with an agreement with Alitalia. Thrust reversers deployed, one of Alitalia's large fleet of Douglas DC-9s, a late model from the Super 80 series, decelerates after landing.

Above: After reorganising its finances in the 1990s, Sabena joined forces with Swissair and Delta. The Belgian carrier bought twelve 85-seat Avro RJ85 quadrijets in 1996, followed by two more in 1997 and nine larger RJ100s (100 seats). These extremely quiet aircraft, developed from the Hawker Siddeley HS-146 designed twenty years ago, are used on Sabena's short-haul routes.

Above: Martinair, the Dutch charter airline specialising in long-haul flights and cargo transport, operates a number of Boeing 767-300ER aircraft. Of the three Dutch charter airlines, Martinair was the largest. The airline became part of the KLM group in 1998.

Below: For flights to popular holiday destinations in the Mediterranean region and the Canary Islands, the remaining independent Dutch charter carrier Air Holland operates a small fleet of Boeing 737s and Boeing 757s.

Above: Traffic congestion is by no means limited to road traffic. Hub-and-spokes operations have contributed towards a shortage of airspace, terminal and runway slots, especially at peak hours – even at Schiphol.

Above: Some airports have specific problems that cannot be remedied. Schiphol suffers from having a large bird population. As Schiphol offers a large area with little human movement and few natural enemies, it is an attractive spot for birds. After decades of varied attempts to scare off birds failed to produce the desired effect, the new policy is to leave them be, as long as they are on the ground. A birdwatch patrol car speeds past three El Al freighters to check on bird activity along runway 06-24.

Right: Proof that dangers of bird collision are real is this rare photograph of a near miss between a KLM Boeing 737 and two birds. If a bird is sucked into the engine during take-off, the aircraft would have to return to Schiphol for an emergency landing.

Below: With full flaps, an Icelandair Boeing 757 slows down to taxying speed before turning off to the terminal building to deliver its load. Amsterdam and Luxembourg are two favourite destinations of the Icelandic carrier, from where it picks up budget passengers for services across the Atlantic via Reykjavik.

Above: Pushback completed, the ground crew is about to unhook the push-bar from the nosewheel of this Malev Fokker 70. After this, the engines may be started.

Left: The sun catches the nose of this Hungarian Airlines' Fokker 70 as it is prepared for pushback from gate G2. All modern aircraft are equipped with special plug-in sockets for communication with the ground crew.

Right: The hub-and-spokes system means minimising connecting times, and reducing passenger waiting time as much as feasible. While the midday wave is about to arrive, passengers bide their time at one of Schiphol's coffee corners that offer a view of the apron. In the background the first of a number of KLM UK flights, a Fokker 100 from Birmingham still bearing the Air UK colour scheme, has arrived at gate D25.

Opposite above: After KLM, Air UK is Schiphol's biggest user, offering flights to some fourteen destinations in the British Isles, giving substance to Schiphol's often repeated claim of being 'London's Third Airport'. A Fokker 100 after landing on a rainy day.

Opposite below: After more than a decade of a dark blue and grey livery, British Airways has adopted a new corporate image. Artists from the various countries to which BA offers services are invited to provide decorative designs for individual aircraft from its fleet. A Boeing 737-300 was photographed taxying to its parking stand at Schiphol.

Above: This British Midland Fokker 70 was photographed about to turn off runway 06 towards Schiphol's two control towers. In the second half of the 1980s Schiphol initiated a plan for considerable expansion of its terminal facilities and for the construction of commercial office buildings in the central area of the airport. As a result, the old control tower (to the right) was no longer high enough to offer a clear view of all areas of the airport and a new 101-metre high tower was built. It became operational in 1991.

Opposite above: Since the British and Dutch Governments signed an agreement in 1984 for complete liberalisation of air services between the two countries, there has been much competition on the air routes across the North Sea. In 1996 Easy Jet was the latest addition, offering services between Schiphol, Luton and Liverpool. The new carrier cut costs by not issuing tickets, like other airlines do, but entering all bookings that come in by telephone directly into its computer system.

Opposite below: In the uncertain wintry morning light, Polskie Linie Lotnicze (LOT) flight LO268 departs from runway 09 for its flight to Warsaw. LOT operates Boeing 737-400 and 737-500 aircraft on the route to Amsterdam.

Below: Air Lanka flight UL563 from Colombo was photographed about to touchdown on runway 06. The aircraft is an Airbus A340, the latest long-range jet to come out of the Toulouse-based European aircraft manufacturing conglomerate. Note how the rear wheels slope downwards for a cushioned landing.

Above: Once at the terminal and having shed its passengers, an array of cargo is unloaded from the A340, which was designed to replace the older versions of the Boeing 747.

Below: As another A340 approaches pushback, the airport ground crew unhooks the 400 Hz electrical system, which is then pushed downwards into the platform to offer a clean manoeuvring area for the pushback tender.

Above: Kuwait Airways flight KU111 is ready to start up its engines and continue its flight from Kuwait City via Amsterdam to Chicago's O'Hare International Airport.

Above: Among the airlines which use Schiphol as a staging point for intercontinental flights between America and the Middle East is Royal Jordanian Airlines. For this type of operation, Schiphol's efficiency in rapid turn-around is important. Here, Royal Jordanian's Lockheed L-1011-500 *Princess Zeina*, which has arrived from New York, is refuelled from Schiphol's underground hydrant system ready for its midday flight to Amman.

Below: Elsewhere, cargo is assembled for a Martinair flight to Miami. Over the past decades cargo has become increasingly important for both scheduled and non-scheduled operations.

Below: Assorted passenger baggage is loaded onto a conveyor belt which reaches up to the rear cargo hold of Martinair's Boeing 767-300ER *Queen Beatrix*. Meanwhile, a catering truck has pulled up and raised its load level with the aircraft's rear door.

Below: Passengers who have passed through Customs can relax in the spacious tax-free shopping centre, available (from 1999) to those travelling outside the European Union.

Above: The sun is reflected off Malaysia Airlines' Boeing 777-200. Malaysia received this particular aircraft, its first Boeing 777, in April 1977 after it set the Speed Around the World, Eastbound record. It flew Seattle –Kuala Lumpur–Seattle, a distance of 23,000 miles, in 41 hours and 59 minutes. Malaysia's Triple Seven, which carries 278 passengers, is the IGW (Increased Gross Weight) version of the long-range twin-jet and has a maximum take-off weight of 317,600lb (144,060kg). Nevertheless, two pairs of six wheels are enough to support the plane.

Opposite: As the time of departure approaches, a final check is made around Martinair's *Queen Beatrix*, making certain that all is clear for pushback.

Above: Malaysia flight MH17 to Kuala
Lumpur is readied for engine start-up. In
1998 Malaysia's fast-growing airline joined
the KLM/Northwest alliance.

Opposite: Also bound for the Far East is
this Thai Airways International MD-11
receiving cargo in its forward cargo bay.
To ensure that the valuable goods sent by
air stay dry during loading and unloading
each aircraft pallet is wrapped in plastic.
Thai uses plastic in its own colours.

Right: As the aircraft is refuelled for its single-stop flight to Bangkok, a lone aircraft container awaits its turn to be loaded into the rear cargo hold. Meanwhile, inside the terminal passengers are assembled in the boarding area at gate G8.

Below: Not all aircraft stands have fuel hydrants. Planes parked at remote stands, such as this Taiwanese Eva Air MD-11, will be fuelled from the customary low-slung fuel trucks.

Below: KLM's McDonnell Douglas MD-11 *Maria Montessori* makes an impressive sight as the aircraft is moved from one of the remote parking stands near Schiphol's new Cargo Southeast facility to the central terminal area.

Above: Waiting for permission to cross runway 06-24, KLM's new aircraft tugs lift the front wheels of the MD-11 off the ground and lock them with a special mechanism. This eases the process of moving and steering the big jet while on tow.

Left: Arriving from Jakarta, Garuda Indonesia's MD-11 slowly approaches the terminal area after landing on runway 19R.

Below: For the Boeing 747-400, lifting the front wheels for ground manoeuvring is not yet an option. Special pushbars and heavy vehicles are necessary to move the 385,000 kg 'Jumbo'.

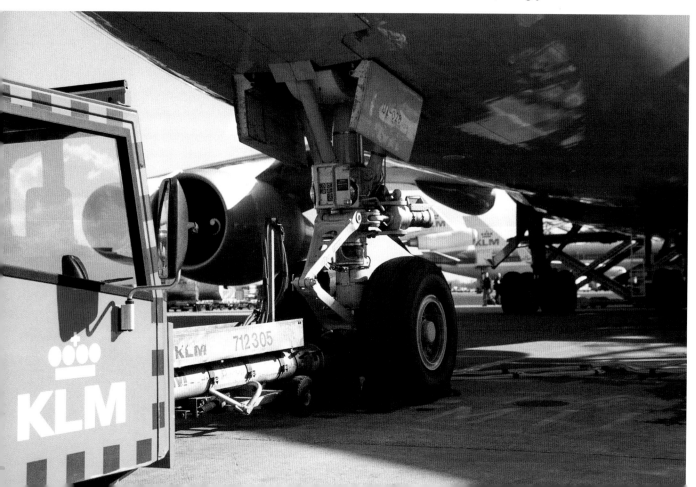

Below: Slowly and carefully, a Boeing 747-400 is moved back from the gate to engine start-up position.

Above: An airline alliance at work – after taking on cargo, a KLM MD-11 is moved to its gate to receive passengers, luggage and fuel for its code-shared flight KL625/NBW8625 to Memphis, Tennessee.

Right: With a two-hour delay, Garuda flight GA994 arrives at its designated gate, nearly twenty-four hours after pushback at Jakarta's Soekarno-Hatta Airport. A number of its passengers will report to the transfer desks inside the terminal to arrange their onward journey.

Below: As the afternoon proceeds, a
VARIG Brazilian Airlines' MD-11 arrives
from São Paulo and Rio de Janeiro.

Opposite below: For an airport like Schiphol, which relies so much on transfer passengers, an efficient system of baggage handling is of crucial importance to minimise turn-around times. In the 1980s substantial amounts of money were invested in an automated baggage system, known by its Dutch acronym BAS. It has since been expanded and updated to cope with the growing number of passengers. Optical bar code readers feed flight/destination and gate information into a computer, which steers each conveyor belt trolley, and the suitcase on it, to its proper collection point.

The baggage handling system achieves high operating speeds, as distances between gates are considerable at Schiphol. At their appropriate destination gate, the trolleys tip their bags onto a slide, from where they are transported to the aircraft in the 'baggage train'.

Opposite above: In the wintry afternoon sun, a KLM Boeing 737-300 is about to touch down on runway 01R. In the background can be seen the flight hangars of the former Fokker factory which have been deserted since the company's bankruptcy in 1996.

Opposite below: The airport's skyline offers an interesting sight at dusk.

Above: Cargo is assembled for one of KLM's evening flights departing from B-pier.

Left: About to depart for a non-stop flight to Singapore, this KLM Boeing 747-400 awaits the all-clear signal from the ground crew before starting up its engines.

Opposite above: Early morning at the apron of Schiphol East, the site of the original airport which is now used to park corporate jets.

Opposite below: On a typically bleak Dutch morning, a Singapore Airlines' Boeing 747-400 is boarding passengers at gate G7.

Above: Northwest's recently acquired Boeing 747-400 makes a colourful sight against the sky. The long line of empty cargo flatbeds indicate the aircraft's loading process is nearly complete.

Above: Under a forbidding grey sky a Korean Airlines cargo plane taxies to Schiphol's Cargo Station Southwest. Korean is one of the airlines which has converted its older Boeing 747s to full freighter configuration.

Opposite above: A relic of the 1960s, this Lebanese Trans Mediterranean Airways' (TMA) Boeing 707 has also been converted into a full freighter. TMA has been a long-standing customer at Schiphol, although tightening of noise restrictions and the introduction of landing surcharges for noisy aircraft have made the airport less attractive for cargo operations with first-generation jets.

Below: This photograph demonstrates the loading of one of El Al's Boeing 747-200F nose loaders at the Aero Groundservices cargo station. In the early 1960s the Boeing 747 project originated in a US Air Force design competition for a large cargo aircraft, won by Lockheeds' design for the C-5. Nonetheless, the Boeing 747 design retained a provision to incorporate a hinged nose section for easy loading. Using the Boeing 747 as a cargo aircraft, however, does require some extra precautions. At the extreme left of the photograph a tail support is visible, necessary to balance the aircraft as the nose section is unloaded.

Below: Loading completed, this El Al freighter taxies to runway 09 for take-off. El Al is a big cargo customer for Schiphol, operating several cargo flights a day.

Left: Schiphol has three cargo areas. Here a Transavia Boeing 737 lands in front of the latest facility, Cargo Southeast, opened early in 1998.

Below: Schiphol is one of Europe's prime airports for air cargo. This line-up of freighters at cargo Station Southwest includes Mandarin Airlines from Taiwan, KLM, South African Airways and Malaysian.

Opposite: Another frequent cargo customer at Schiphol is Iran Air, which operates a scheduled cargo service between Tehran and Schiphol. The tanks in the background are the airport's main fuel depot.

Below: A view inside Iran Air's cargo machine, halfway through unloading at Avia Presto's Cargo Station Southeast. All cargo pallets are secured to the floor of the aircraft, equipped with an electrically operated conveyor mechanism to move the pallets to their proper position.

Below: Weighed down with a full load, this Nippon Cargo Airlines plane is rolling towards the motorway overpass to reach runway 01L for take-off to Japan in the late afternoon.

Below: A KLM Asia Boeing 747-400 taxies to its holding position before take-off. To avoid diplomatic controversies with China over air services between Amsterdam and Taipei, KLM founded a daughter company in Taiwan, KLM Asia, which leases aircraft and crews from KLM in Holland. Note the absence of the customary crown symbol above the KLM logo.

Above: Delta Air Lines' flight 38 from Atlanta taxies to its gate at Schiphol's G-pier, which handles intercontinental flights. Delta is gradually replacing its fleet of ageing Lockheed L-1011-500 TriStars with extended range Boeing 767s.

Below: United, operating the Boeing 777 between Washington's Dulles Airport and Schiphol, is one of three American carriers which offer scheduled services to Amsterdam.

Below: Empty seats remain at the clean area near the gate after pushback of a Pakistan International Airways (PIA) Airbus A310-200, leaving for Karachi.

Above: PIA's flight PK724 is about to begin its 16½-hour flight to Karachi, with one stop *en route* to refuel the Airbus.

Below: A Mandarin Airlines MD-11 mixed cargo and passenger aircraft is starting its engines after pushback from the G-pier.

Below: A KLM Cityhopper Fokker 70 photographed showing its old white and dark blue colour scheme, now abandoned in favour of increased KLM brand visibility.

Below: Engines revved and flaps in landing position, this Fokker 70 comes in on runway 27, showing the new Cityhopper colours.

Below: One of Air UK's frequent Fokker 50 commuter flights crosses the threshold of runway 01R on a rainy day.

Left: For passengers arriving on commuter flights, a temporary pier has been constructed in advance of plans to extend the terminal in a south-westerly direction. Here too the large windows that are so characteristic of Schiphol abound, offering a good view of the activity on the apron.

Below: Touchdown – tyres blow off smoke as they hit the runway and start to roll. This KLM Boeing 737-300 has made another safe landing, delivering its passengers in time for the airline's afternoon 'wave' of connecting flights.

Below: Hub-and-spokes operations inevitably involve extra waiting time for passengers. Schiphol offers its passengers various ways to pass the time: from working in the Business Centre's rental office facilities, to shopping, visiting the casino, or simply reading in the relaxed environment of the airport's upper deck.

Below: For the hurried traveller who is only passing through the airport, even the typical scenario of the Amsterdam canals and a 'brown café' has been recreated. In the best of Dutch traditions, the bicycle is chained and padlocked to the railing outside the café.

Right: One of KLM's new Boeing 767-300ERs takes off from runway 01L. The red and white pole in the foreground contains noise monitoring equipment. Controlling noise levels is one of the challenges facing Schiphol.

Below: At gate G4 the catering truck has arrived for Delta's flight 81 to New York's John F. Kennedy Airport, flown by a Boeing 767-300ER. KLM was not the only airline to benefit from the open skies accord between the Netherlands and the USA in 1992. Atlanta-based Delta Air Lines appeared victorious from the reshuffling of the US airline industry that went on in the 1980s, and expanded its transatlantic services to Europe by introducing a new operating concept: Extended Twin-engined Operations (ETOPS in aviation jargon).

Above: An Iran Air Airbus A300 rolls to its
designated gate at the G-pier to deliver its
Holland-bound and transfer passengers.

Right: With engines at maximum power, this Icelandair Boeing 757 lifts off to begin its flight to Reykjavik Airport.

Below: A Royal Air Maroc Boeing 737 illustrates the size of the new Sheraton Hotel and Amsterdam Airport World Trade Centre.

Below: An Air UK Fokker 100 prepares to roll for a late flight to its home base at London-Stansted.

Above: Towards midnight, when most scheduled services have stopped and a relative calm descends on the airport, scores of empty baggage trolleys stand idle in the assembly area in front of the E-pier.

Key figures for Amsterdam Airport Schiphol

Principal Results for 1997

Commercial Traffic	1997	1998	
Commercial aircraft movements	349,500	377,000	(+ 7.8%)
Passengers (millions)	31.6	34.4	(+ 9.0%)
Cargo transport (million tonnes)	1.161	1.160	(- 0.1%)

Financial Results

Turnover (million guilders)	1,104.9
Net profit (million guilders)	246.8